FINISHING LINE PRESS

www.finishinglinepress.com

10 Hours to Tulsa

poems by

Shelley Nation

Finishing Line Press
Georgetown, Kentucky

10 Hours to Tulsa

ACKNOWLEDGMENTS

"9 Hours to Tulsa" published by *Exact Change Only Magazine*
"Rueben" published by *The Dead Mule School of Southern Literature*
"The Trailer Next Door" published by *Wisconsin Review*
"Single Mother", "Stepfather", "Tonya", "The Visit" published by *Litbreak Magazine*

Publisher: Leah Huete de Maines
Editor: Christen Kincaid
Cover Art: Camilla McGinty
Author Photo: Kelly Anquoe
Cover Design: Elizabeth Maines McCleavy

Order online: www.finishinglinepress.com
also available on amazon.com

Author inquiries and mail orders:
Finishing Line Press
PO Box 1626
Georgetown, Kentucky 40324
USA

Contents

10 Hours To Tulsa

Her dreams were like fantasies
knotted up intestinal tract thoughts.
Shoving painkillers into painful memories
she washed them clean with bottled spirits
and kept driving.

Remembered images drew themselves
like maps along the dashboard
each intense pattern neglecting
forensic evidence of her past.
She wiped the dust clean
and kept driving.

Each steering wheel spoke
bent along her fingers, spiraling into
rows of trailer park dreams
it seemed she would never get out
wondered why she would ever return.

Her redneck philosophy did not
meld with her civilized tongue
remembered her father asking,
what does Chicago have
that you can't get here,
she ground the gears into fifth
and kept driving.

Ten hours to Tulsa
Ten hours left to scream along the asphalt
flung her desires out the open window
watched remnants of her father's dream
skid off the highway into mud-filled ditches
she only wishes she didn't belong.

Rudy

His broad shoulders held up his neck that rotated
impulsively toward his son's girlfriends,
might miss a great piece of ass,
tight mini-skirts from early sixties fashion.

His feet lodged in pointed cowboy boots,
held up is 6 ft., 2 in. frame,
shoes filled to the tips with newspaper
ever since that freight train wheel
severed the tips of his toes.

His bulky belt buckle held up his trousers
with pockets perfect for housing flasks
filled with gin, whiskey, rum to numb his mind
of witchery wife who found holy waters wasteland,
no more dancin' and drinkin' on a Saturday night,
not for her.

His '55 Chevy drove him to the bars
to drink away sobriety,
daughter waiting in the front seat late at night,
feet barely reaching the pedals
making sure daddy gets home safe.

Single Mother

She was airlifted out of Muskogee
with 200 dollars in her pocket
and a small child under each arm.

Bosses hired her as a secretary for sale
sent her home each Christmas with a box
full of sausages, hard cheeses and seed filled crackers.

Boyfriends crawled out from under
steel enforced frames ready for arm-twisting
dates and threatening stances.

Apartments allowed a sort of recluse
from outside barbarity until the woman
from upstairs began screaming for her sanity,
and moving became necessary,
again.

Neighborhood children created
an atmosphere of terror
screaming at her babies that the devil's going to get them
and booger eating people were going to hell.

Bouffant hair teased to the quick promised showers
of hairspray rain causing hands to flip
invisible objects off her shoulders,
a forest given to hiding bobby pins perfect
for opening doors locked by temper tantrum children.

She touched down on an idea
far removed from her dream,
created memories for small children
to swallow as their own.

The Trailer Next Door

Rows of metal meat cans filled with Jerry Falwell dreams
she screams bleach blond hair rich black roots
tight blue jeans riding around her hips
she dips to the country music blasting in her brain
Her life is centered around
front yard weed gardens
rotting furniture, ½ a minute from total decomposition
a miracle created in a sordid lifestyle of delusions
She breathes for cheap weed, easy back-seat fucks
rusted out trucks,
the main stays of Friday night juke-joint dances
where every night is a chance to get away in her mind
create a new form of herself,
running around in the rags pulled from dead-end
nightmares

She pleads for someone to use her body
fling it against metal vibrating posts stuck in the ground
holding her breath she screams "This is my destiny!
This is my purpose to live amongst brain dead fetuses!"
singing Hank Williams lyrics with the rhythm of her ass
thrusting against the walls of her double-wide
cigarette lounging on her lower lip
she sips from a bottle of bourbon, shakes her tits a little more
to reassure Billy Bob she is having the time of her life

Uncle Harry

yeah, at 65 I still bleach my hair
wear a large cowboy hat on my head
giant belt buckle 'round my waist and a
chewed up toothpick 'tween my lips

first wife, donna, 'came a lesbian
lives with ruth in the doublewide down the street
first child, dina's got the schizophrenia,
keeps goin' off her meds to have my grandkids
last time she smashed the bathroom mirror,
cut herself up real bad
tryin to safe herself from someone livin in her head

second kid's randy
worked a spell as a roadie with dwight yokam
'til the heroin and cocaine got to be too much
now he's settlin down with some chick he met
10 years older an him, got two lil ones
guess he's a daddy now too

dad died few years back
yeah, he's in a better place and all, now
'way from that crazy ol' wife o' his
kept him drinkin all those years
hidin' flasks all 'round the whole damn trailer
maybe it'll be a little easier findin'
myself a new lady,
don't have to be worrin' bout him pinchin'
their asses ever time i bring a new one aroun'

but me, well, you know always have been
a lady's man, guess i do get that from the ol' man
fin'ly did get hitched again 'bout thirty years
or so ago

second wife, deb, blonde hair, black roots
six kids, all of em kinda hazy with
mary jane smells fillin' up the entire double-wide
not a one of 'em had a inch of inclination to
do nothin', spendin' all my money,
smokin' up my weed, drinkin' all my booze
an' deb thinkin' all the while it's okay
came from her, her lil babies, least they
ain't killin' no one she says
well, I got tired a that shit
after twenty years, threw her out
with the entire crew of her babies,
grandbabies, had a whole zoo livin' with me

now I just hang around, datin' here
an' there, bein' my own man, doin' my
own thing, I get along nicely by myself

well, it's time for me to move on,
got a few more stops to make 'fore I
gotta put this here truck to bed
don't be a stranger, always have enough
beer in the fridge to share with a neighbor

The Visit

As a 5 year old child
Made to stay with stranger father
Shrinking from stepmother drudgery
She screams "Sit on your daddy's lap!"
But my daddy's back in Tulsa
The one who made me come to this broken-down farm
Where chicks get under my feet
And are crushed dead
I'm yelled at for killing the yellow fluff
Who quacks and is forever quiet
Where a cow steps backward crushing my toe
Eliciting sharp pain-again it is my fault
For placing my foot where it doesn't belong
And it dawns on me that I don't belong
In this town on this farm with a stranger
Who says he is my father

La Petite

I was 3
my crying,
a mystery train bound
for isolation,
pacified only with an Oreo cookie.

I was 3
urine wet,
chafed and waiting
riding a springing hippo
watching daddies board the daycare depot;
here to pick up
a son, a daughter.

Alone, damp,
jealous
why couldn't I have a daddy,
who dries my tears,
makes me laugh,
saves me from monsters,
takes me home.

Tonya

She and I were aliens from another world
Her large black mutt was the master king we served
Our faces for the outer world were disguises
We showed our true form only to each other in a ruse
Of face gestures, hands swept across our features.
At bedtime, during stay-overs,
Listerine became gin
Bathroom doors stayed locked as we kept our mouths full
Pretended to savor the taste of liquor
The sink counter, our night-time bar and place
Where we picked up our men.
Bicycle rides were times to transport
Our imaginary children from school to our homes.
Hopefully her mother would be absent
And we would sit at the kitchen table sipping
Kool-aide as coffee, discussing problems with our children
Messed up marriages and disappointed dreams.
Eventually her family moved away.
Her popularity did not fit with our plans of creativity;
I was forced to become the only living alien
The barfly at the counter
The disappointed mother.
Eventually I had to grow up too.

The River

The river fills her with energy,
episodes of triangular wisdom.

She expresses enunciated challenges,
knows when to drown emotions
like whirlpools of questions sliding beneath the surface.

Suddenly she understands the *Dakwa's despair,
the suppressed rage of mambas.

She will acknowledge what others reject,
let her arms tighten around
objects, as liquid as that 32 oz. soda
she drinks every day.

The river has become
a wasteland for her memories
piling one atop the other.

Each child is a separate line in an autopsy
that ends in drowning,
and if nothing else,
makes her step backwards,
away from foaming waters.

Fingerprints slowly fade from fingertips
becoming new clouds over a land of childhood disasters.
The +Tlanusi'yi will drown her on the ledge
while she contemplates her life,
her anger evaporating through olive skin.
She will never acknowledge that she exists,
shove her arms into twisted bailing wire,
rough and metallic,
splitting atoms,
dividing creation.

*The Dakwa was a large mythical fish that lived in the Tennessee River eating humans until a great hunter got swallowed by him and figured out a way to cut him open to save himself and hence kill the great fish.

+The Tlanusi'yi is a great leech with red and white stripes along its body who lives in Valley River under a ledge of rock. Whenever people sit on the rock, the Tlanusi'yi thrashes about causing a large spray of white water to come up and drown them.

Unmentionables

Sister dared me to throw my panties
across the room
her on the top bunk
me on the bottom
Even then I knew
it wasn't proper
Knew my privates
should be kept private
Knew my tiny nighty
would not cover it all

Mom couldn't figure out why
I wouldn't come from under the covers
to meet her new date,
standing in the doorway.

Tornado alley

A 5 year old at dinner
Restaurant empty
Streets deserted
Ochre sky
Trees unwavering
Ordering her favorite meal
Waiters slightly annoyed
Not being able to go home to
Protect their families
Even at 5, she feels the danger
Knows she should be home
Protected
Her family leaves,
Car trip home
Watches the garage door
Slowly close
But not before sighting a
Gray, brown funnel
Hovering, above the asphalt
Easing its way towards her

A Friend from Bartlesville Comes to Visit

After all the board games had been played,
the gossip released from lips,
and the dog thoroughly tortured,
the only thing left to do was snoop
inside my mother's dresser.

Beneath a pile of folded satin panties,
my name written on a small white envelope
stunned me into silence.

I finally told my friend
"It's okay if I open it,
it was written to me anyway,"
as I lifted it out of the drawer,
a letter hidden from me.
Seeing it was from my stepfather,
I slid my finger along the
Flap of the envelope.

He begged me to believe him;
that he did not punch
Julie ten times in the face,
says it didn't happen that way.
Wanted me to know he wasn't the boogey man;
would never hurt us,
asked me to choose sides,
begged me to write back.

Slowly, I replaced the letter
beneath the satin panties,
closed the drawer,
slowly slipped outside
with my friend
beneath the sun.

Storm Clouds

They screamed at one another
Let anger rise, created storm clouds
Hovering up along the ceiling in their house
She raged to her room
Her Dad out the back door

Hours later
She drifted into the air
Saw him hunched in the driver's seat
created words in her head of apologies
That fell into the grass as she approached
Brain matter splattered along the back window

She spun
floated back to the house
in a daze of not understanding
of imagining that time had stopped
with a mind that can't feel any longer
slowly climbed into bed and
slept

Stepfather

1

My sister and I linked together,
sharing a tremble between us,
walking toward hell after school,
unknowing whether the demon
will be visiting our house,
or maybe he'll be at work
and we're safe turning this corner
until 6 o'clock madness.

2

3,4,5 times around the table,
he grabs her hair and pulls back,
eyes red with vacant look.
Her mother screams,
her stepfather ignores
and punches her in the face
6 times.
If only she had gotten off that damn couch,
even though she had worked for twelve hours
at the amusement park.
She was tired, achy,
found release in fleece blanket,
"Can't we do it in the morning?" she begged.
He stood over her trembling,
not understanding how someone could deny him-
not given into his demands-
would not surrender to his power-
so she became a flower being plucked,
petals falling with each punch.
Somehow, in the core of her body,
her mother freed her from the demon,
pulled her to safety out the backdoor,
into the neighbor's yard,

down the street and to the front bell
where I sat with neighborhood children.
If only she had gotten off that damn couch
and checked the oil.

3

Entombed, my sister and I,
in bathroom darkness,
our stepfather screams at our mother
through my own screams
"I want my daddy!"
Telephone, shoes, hangers,
hit the shut door,
the entrance to their room.
Rivers from my eyes stain
a pink Easter dress,
worn for this day.

Everclear

Everclear, not the band, 5 years before that
And another drink, strawberries at the bottom
Catching fruit between teeth through laughter
I'm engaging, constant chatter, swirling
I am dancing, stopping in mid-sentence
"Let me go oooooon" Violent Femmes crooning
Slam dance motion
And another drink, strawberries gone,
And another drink, friends disappearing,
And another drink, walking along alleys
Strange man along my side
Stepping sideways, clumsy, faltering footsteps
Another drink, looking at the clear skies
Pinned on the ground, groaning to find words
Slurred speech, unrecognizable language
A mannequin without limbs,
Pushing against air, fog invading thoughts
I hear shouts, threats, the body above me
becomes airborne
A friend pulls me off the ground
I am nestled into his car,
my guardian angel

Shelley Nation was the co-host of one of Chicago's longest running poetry talk shows, *Wordslingers*, which aired on WLUW FM from Loyola University, from 1999 to 2009. She has been writing and performing poetry in the Chicago area since 1988, and has hosted several poetry venues over the years. She has been published in many poetry journals including *Wisconsin Review, The Dead Mule School of Southern Literature, The RavenPerch, Copperfield Review Quarterly,* among others. Shelley has been a teacher and counselor in Chicago for the past 31 years and holds two Master's Degrees in education. Shelley is a citizen of the Cherokee Nation of Oklahoma and has recently begun to write about the experience of her grandmother and other members of her family as they lived through their struggles in Cherokee Nation territory, from Tennessee and Alabama to the Canadian District in Indian Territory/Oklahoma.